MORE
MONOLOGUES
FOR
KIDS

Ruth Mae Roddy

Dramaline Publications
10470 Riverside, Drive, Suite #201
Toluca Lake, CA 91602
818/985-9148
Fax: 818/985-0408

Cover Art: John Sabel

This book is printed on 55# Glatfelter acid-free paper. A paper that meets the requirements of the American Standard of Permanence of paper for printed library material.

CONTENTS

GIRLS

WORK SHEET

DIANE

Diane and her parents disagree regarding music.

My mom and dad are really lame when it comes to music. They want me to listen to all this dumb stuff that no kid in the world would ever listen to. Unless he was tied down or locked up in a room or something and couldn't get away from it. When they play their old records I have to hold my ears.

Most of the stuff they like makes me sick. Stuff by people I've never ever heard of. People like Kenny Rogers, and Smokey Robinson, and Barbra Streisand, and a bunch of old-timey people like that. Hey, I mean, who wants to listen to Barbra Streisand, anyway?

Face it, most parents are pretty dopey when it comes to music. They expect you to like the stuff they liked when they were growing up. They don't understand that the music kids like today is a whole lot neater and a lot cooler than the old, sappy, outdated junk they used to listen to. Even the Beatles. They're out of date, too. Even though some of their songs aren't so bad. But they didn't dance or even have videos. Hey, music isn't any fun unless you can see it.

Come to think of it, though, who'd want to see Kenny Rogers?

WORK SHEET

_____

_____

_____

_____

_____

_____

_____

_____

_____

_____

BARBARA

Barbara doesn't understand disloyalty.

Sometimes it seems like your friends go out of their way to be creepy. To do stuff that's mean and cruel and hurts your feelings.

Like Doris Hamilton. She's my best friend. We play together almost every day and hang around in school together and do stuff together on the weekends. It seems like we're always together, you know. She's either here at my house or I'm over at hers.

I like Doris a lot. But last week when she went to the amusement park, she didn't ask me to go along. She asked Sheri Johnson to go instead. And after all the things we do for her, too. Last summer we took her along on our vacation. And when we go on trips and picnics and stuff, we always take her with us.

She'd been acting really funny all last week. Like kind of weird, you know. And now I understand why. Because she was being sneaky, that's why. Because she knew all along she was going to ask Sheri to go with her instead of me. She knew she was being a rat.

I wonder why people can't be honest and just tell you the truth instead of being weasels. I wonder how come being honest is so hard?

5

WORK SHEET

RUTH

Ruth is upset by her parent's divorce.

My mom and dad got divorced last summer. They hadn't been getting along so good for a long time. They'd been arguing a lot and yelling bad things at each other and making all kinds of noise the neighbors could hear. Or they wouldn't talk to each other for days. I think that was even worse than all the yelling. When they didn't talk it was awful. Just being in the same room with them gave you the creeps.

A long time ago, a couple of years back, my parents got along okay. They used to be nice to each other and kiss each other and it was really good living with them. Then—something happened and everything changed. I'm not sure what. They don't say much about it.

My dad moved away to another part of town and my mom sold our house. Now the three of us—my mom, my brother and I—live in an apartment.

I see my dad once a week. He picks me up on Wednesdays. And I spend every other weekend with him, too. And we have a good time. But it's still not like it was before.

I don't like being a part-time kid.

WORK SHEET

MARY

It's no fun watching what you eat.

My mom is all the time yelling at me about what I eat. To the point where I can't eat anything anymore. This is because she's afraid I'll get fat. "Don't eat burgers, Mary!" "Don't eat French fries, Mary!" "Don't drink milkshakes, Mary!" I mean, hey, after all, if a person can't eat fries and burgers and shakes, what's the sense of living, you know.

She's always fixing me salads and all this diet stuff that doesn't have any flavor. Some of the junk tastes like you're chewing on wood, or something, you know. And, hey, nobody likes salads, do they? Not really. Except maybe old people like my mom and dad.

I think Mom doesn't want me to eat so much because she's overweight and she's afraid I'll get like that, too. She's kind of on the fat side, you know. She's always telling her best friend, Betty, about how she's gained all this weight and how her clothes don't fit anymore and how she's going on a diet. It seems like she's always on a diet. Except she's always sneaking potato chips and ham sandwiches and stuff like that —stuff with flavor.

I guess maybe *she* hates lettuce, too.

WORK SHEET

_____

_____

_____

_____

_____

_____

_____

_____

_____

_____

_____

PAM

Personal hygiene should not be overdone.

My mother makes me take a bath every day. Every day. Whether I need one or not. And I'm not even dirty, either. A person can't get dirty in just one day. It takes a long time to get dirty. But she always makes me take a shower or a bath, anyway. And if I don't, she'll yell at me and give me one herself. Which is really awful. Because this means that I have to get rubbed so hard my skin hurts. Mom scrubs me like I'm the kitchen sink or something.

And she digs in my ears real hard, too. And she always gets soap in my eyes. And if I say anything, she always says that I shouldn't be such a baby. Hey, how would she like it if some great big person stuck their fingers in her eyes and ears?

The worst part is getting my hair washed. Because this always means you have to get your face all wet and have your head rubbed so hard you wanna cry. And then she combs it out. Wow! This is the worst part of all. Because she combs it real rough to get the tangles and stuff out and almost pulls my head off. The last time she combed my hair she combed out a whole big wad of it. It hurt so bad I screamed.

I don't think the reason they wanna give you baths and wash your hair is to get you clean. I think it's just another excuse to be mean.

WORK SHEET

_____

_____

_____

_____

_____

_____

_____

_____

_____

_____

_____

ELLEN

Family get-togethers are a special time.

My very best special thing in the whole world is when my family gets together. Especially at my grandmother's and grandfather's house.

When we do, everybody brings some kind of food. My mom usually brings salads because this is what she makes the best. My Aunt Julie always brings baked beans. Aunt Sally brings a cake. Everybody brings something. This way my grandmother doesn't have to do all the cooking.

We have to have extra chairs and stuff because there are so many of us we all can't eat at the same table. And it's always real crowded and noisy when all of us get together, too. But this is the good part—all of us being together, that is. It's a really neat time with everybody talking and eating and having fun.

My grandfather always tells these same old jokes that my grandmother thinks are sappy. But this is what makes them so funny—that they're really dumb and corny. I could listen to him tell them over and over.

When we're all together it's a special time and it makes me feel good inside. Being part of a big family is one of the nicest things a kid can have.

WORK SHEET

_____

_____

_____

_____

_____

_____

_____

_____

_____

_____

_____

FRANCIE

Street people just can't be ignored.

Near our house is a service station. We go there to get gas. When we do, we see these people who look like tramps or something. Their clothes are all grubby and torn and they wear shoes that are broken open and all run over. They hang around the place and ask people for money.

At first I was scared of them because they looked weird, you know. And I used to scoot down in the seat of our car so they wouldn't see me. But then my dad said that there wasn't anything to be afraid of. He said that they were homeless people with no place to go. He said that I shouldn't be afraid of them, that instead I should feel sorry for them because they are poor and on the streets without a roof over their heads. He said I should understand that not all people live like we do, that a lot of people in this world are hungry and cold and that every day for them is a hard time.

When we go to the service station now, I don't hide anymore. Instead, I smile at the people and they smile back. And, once in a while, Daddy gives me money to give them.

Now, instead of being afraid, I just think about how lucky I am.

WORK SHEET

_____

_____

_____

_____

_____

_____

_____

_____

_____

_____

_____

ELSIE

Elsie has adjusted to her family's plight.

My father used to work at the Harris Tractor Company. They made these big tractors for farmers and stuff. He had a good job and had people working for him. Then, alluva sudden like, they closed the factory down. Now Daddy's out of work.

Daddy has been looking for something else to do for a long time, but he can't seem to find anything good. So he's been working part-time at Miller's Hardware store. The only thing is, we don't have money like we used to when he was working at the tractor place. And this means we have to be careful.

My mom is helping out by working at the Kmart and my brother, Richard, he got a job at the supermarket. Everybody is pitching in. I'm the only one who isn't working because I'm too young. But I do stuff to help out around the house so my mother won't have so much to do when she's home.

I vacuum the carpets and dust and clean and even change the sheets on the beds. This is the hardest job of all because you have to keep running back and forth around the bed.

Sometimes I think not having everything you want is okay. It makes you realize how important your family can be.

WORK SHEET

FLORA

She has strong feelings regarding her mother's dating.

After my mother and father got a divorce, my mom and I were together all of the time. We did all kinds of neat stuff together. It was like we were sisters, or something, you know. It was fun and it was the best time I ever had.

Then, alluva sudden, she goes and starts dating and it's like I never see her anymore, okay? Because she's always going out with these men. And most of them are real geeks, you know.

And when they come to pick up my mom they usually bring me stuff, too. And treat me extra nice. They do this so my mom will think they're okay, so she'll be impressed. And they think I don't know what they're doing, you know. Hey! I mean, like. . . . kids aren't stupid.

This one guy brought me this giant stuffed Snoopy. It was so big he couldn't get it through the front door. Another guy brought me a Game Boy. Most of them try to buy me off with something. But most of them are jerks.

None of them are as neat as my dad. All he has to bring me is himself.

WORK SHEET

_____

_____

_____

_____

_____

_____

_____

_____

_____

_____

_____

BOYS

WORK SHEET

AARON

Dance is not for Aaron.

Last year my mom took me to this dance class because my grandmother said she thought I had rhythm. I don't know how she ever got this idea. I never dance and jump around to music, or anything. But, anyway, she said I had talent, you know.

So, Mom takes me to this dance place where there's this bunch of geeks jumping around like they're walking on fire, or something. It was weird. A whole bunch of kids acting like jerks. And they were jumping around to this stupid classical music that sounded like a bunch of cats when they're hungry.

The girls were all giggling and falling all over each other and the boys looked clumsy and awkward like their shoes were too heavy. And you should have seen what they made them wear, too. Outfits that looked like panty hose. Wow!

I told Mom I wasn't going to take dancing lessons and that was that. I didn't care what happened—even if Dad got mad and yelled at me. But, that night, when Mom told him, he didn't say anything. He just sat there smiling behind his newspaper.

I guess he wouldn't want to dress up in panty hose either.

WORK SHEET

BART

He speaks of summer camp.

Summer camp is cool because you get to do a whole bunch of stuff you can't do at home. Like swim everyday, make neat things, go on hikes, and ride horses—all kinds of fun junk. It sure beats hanging around the house all summer.

Last week we took this nature hike, okay? In this real deep woods that you could hardly see through. In some places it was so thick you couldn't see the sun. A park ranger took us and we were gone most of the day. We saw all kinds of interesting things: An old village where Indians used to live, some big rock caves, and a tree so big it took ten of us holding hands to reach around it.

You get to stay up later at camp, too. And sit around the campfire and talk and tell stories. One of our counselors told this story about how the woods we took our nature hike in is haunted by the ghost of this Indian chief who is still looking for the soldier who killed his brother. It was scary and really freaked me out. So much I couldn't sleep.

I'm looking forward to camp again next year, too. I can't wait.

But if they expect me to go back in those woods again—forget it.

35

WORK SHEET

_____

_____

_____

_____

_____

_____

_____

_____

_____

_____

FRANK

He reflects on the recent funeral of a friend's father.

Mr. McCann was our neighbor. He lived in the house at the corner of Elm and Parkwood. He was a nice guy. I've been like this friend of his son, Jerry, for a long time. Ever since I can remember. And he and Mrs. McCann were good friends with my mom and dad, too.

When Mr. McCann died, my parents asked me if I wanted to go with them to the funeral home. Well, at first I didn't think it was such a good idea. I mean, I'd never seen a dead person before, you know. So, I told them I didn't want to go, okay?

Then I saw Jerry hanging around outside his house. He was different, it seemed. When I asked him about his dad he didn't say anything. He just shrugged his shoulders and looked away. When I asked him if he was going to the funeral home he said he was but that he didn't want to because it would be too sad. So, then—and don't know why—I said I was going too, that I would see him there. And then he smiled.

The funeral home wasn't as bad as I thought it was going to be. And seeing Mr. McCann didn't bother me either. Now I'm glad I went. Because next time I won't be scared. And besides, I learned that doing something nice for a friend is more important than being afraid any day.

WORK SHEET

JAKE

He has mixed feelings about family picnics.

Every now and then we go on picnics. Mostly on Sundays. I guess because Sundays are pretty boring.

We usually go to Snyder Park because it's close by and has picnic tables and these grills where you can cook your stuff. It also has swings and teeter-totters.

Most of the time—to be honest—I'd rather stay home and mess around and watch TV. But my mom and dad won't let me. They say I'm too young to stay home alone. The real reason, I think, is because they hate to see kids have fun. So, I have to go along with my mom and dad and my sister and our dog and usually my grouchy old aunt Helen.

My mom spends all morning fixing baked beans and potato salad. We always have this. It's like if you don't have beans and potato salad in your car they won't let you into the park. And we take hamburgers and hot dogs, too. Which I really like. But not the way my dad grills them. He trashes them by cooking them too long. My grouchy aunt Helen always brings her specialty — creamed spinach. Wow. You wanna barf just looking at it. Our dog won't even eat it and he'll eat anything. And who ever heard of creamed spinach for a picnic, anyhow?

You know what? I can't wait to grow up.

WORK SHEET

RICHARD

Richard reflects on his father's new companion.

My mom and dad got a divorce a year ago. They weren't getting along so good anymore. All they ever did was yell at each other all the time. I used to go into my room and close the door because I hated to hear them argue.

I've been going over to my dad's place every Wednesday and every other weekend. He lives in this neat condo that has a trash compactor. And he's got this giant-sized TV. We watch sports on it and old movies and stuff. I like to be with my dad. And I still do, I guess, but. . . .

The last time I went over to his place he had this woman there—his girlfriend. Her name is Gail. She's a whole lot younger than he is. And she dresses off the wall and has this freaked-out hair. Like maybe she's part of some rock group, or something, you know. But she's kind of pretty, I guess, in this weird kind of way.

We all went to dinner together and then to a movie. Gail was nice and friendly. She asked me a bunch of questions about what I liked and what I was doing in school and stuff. I have to admit, she's pretty neat.

But she'll never be as neat as my mom.

WORK SHEET

PAUL

Paul loves the fast rides at Midway Park.

One of my favorite things is to go to Midway Park. It's got everything. All kinds of neat video games and good stuff to eat and really neat rides. They put in new rides every year. This is because they have to keep up to date. Nobody likes stupid rides like Ferris wheels and merry-go-rounds and old-timey stuff like that anymore. Except my mom. She's afraid of going on anything that's any fun.

Last year they put in this ride called *The Spider.* The Spider is cool. It's the hottest ride in the park. It looks like this giant steel bug, you know. With these tracks going off in all directions. It has a whole bunch of loops and turns and the car you're in goes almost sixty miles an hour. The Spider is awesome. My mom won't even look at it.

The Spider is so neat my dad and I rode it six times in a row. When I got off, my legs were like spaghetti, or rubber, or something. That's how scary it is. "A Thrill a Second," just like they say on the commercials for it on TV.

I finally talked my sister into going on it with me. After the first loop she started screaming and going nuts. When we got off she threw up all over my new Reeboks. Hey, that was more scary than The Spider any day.

WORK SHEET

_____

_____

_____

_____

_____

_____

_____

_____

_____

_____

LARRY

Larry is grateful for being alive.

It happened when my mom and dad I were driving through this real bad rainstorm in Oklahoma.

We were driving along and everything was okay when, alluva sudden, this car comes flying across the divider and hits us. Our car went out of control and we spun around a bunch of times. It was like we were inside of a top or something. And we just kept spinning and spinning until we crashed into this real deep ditch. It was awful.

My mom broke her left leg and her face got cut up pretty bad. My dad broke a bunch of ribs from being pinned under the steering wheel.

They rushed us to this hospital where they operated on us. They put me in a cast that went from my neck to below my waist. A body cast. This is because my back was broken. It turned out I was hurt worse than anybody. They didn't tell me then, but they didn't know if I'd be able to walk anymore.

But, little by little, I got better. Now I'm fine.

While I was sick I had a lot of time to think, you know. About how a lot of stuff you think's important is just a bunch of junk.

WORK SHEET

STANLEY

Cleanliness is okay—within reason.

I do my best to keep my room neat and clean. But as far as my mom is concerned, I never keep it neat and clean enough. She's always complaining and yelling at me because I have stuff lying around. Hey, you can't keep everything in drawers. I mean, nobody's *that* neat. Besides, what's the big deal, anyway? But she's all the time on my case. She says I'm sloppy. She says I take after Dad, that he's always been a slob, too.

My mom's got like this eagle eye for dust, too. She spots it everywhere: Like behind chairs and under beds, on top of dressers—everywhere. Between you and me, sometimes I think she's kinda nuts on the subject, you know. I mean, c'mon, who comes into your house and starts looking under your beds for dust and stuff? Anyway, what's the big deal about dust if you can't see it?

She got real upset at me last week for sticking my bubblegum on the head of my bed. She went ape. Heck, I mean, gee whiz, I only keep it there overnight. I was just saving it till the next day, that's all. It's stupid to throw out good bubblegum when it's only half-chewed.

Hey, I may be sloppy like my dad, but at least I'm not wasteful.

WORK SHEET

LLOYD

He has learned that prejudice is harmful and wrong.

This summer a Japanese family moved into our neighborhood. They moved into the old Miller place on the corner. And they had a kid my age.

When I told my friends, Ralph and Jimmy, they said I shouldn't play with him because Japanese people are weird. They also said that if I started playing with him they'd stop playing with me. So, I didn't.

I'd see him—his name is John--I'd see him hanging around in his yard a lot. He'd be messing around all by himself. And when he'd come over to the park and hang around where us guys were, everyone would leave. Nobody even spoke to him. For some reason, it made me feel funny.

When I told my dad, he said that treating people bad because they're different than us is an awful thing. He asked me how'd I'd like it if we moved to Japan and nobody spoke to me. I thought about it. It'd be the pits. So, I went over and asked John if he wanted to mess around, and he said, "Yeah."

Now, John and I are best friends and we play together all the time. And Ralph and Jimmy don't speak to me anymore. But I don't care. Because friends like Ralph and Jimmy I don't need.

WORK SHEET

_____

_____

_____

_____

_____

_____

_____

_____

_____

_____

_____

TOM

Tom doesn't enjoy looking after his brother.

One of the things that bugs me the most is having to watch out for my little brother, Bill. He's a real nerd. I'd rather take care of a gorilla for a week than watch out for Billy for ten minutes because he can get into all kinds of stuff and cause a whole lot of trouble real fast.

Mom always leaves Billy with me when we go places and she has to shop. Like she did yesterday when we went to the supermarket. She left the little ape with me, okay? Well, the first thing he does is go and push over this stack of pet food, and cans go rolling all over the place. And when I tried to pick the stuff up he runs off and starts jerking cereal off the shelves. He was like this little buzzsaw going through the store or something.

And when I tried to stop him he yelled at me and started to hit me and go crazy like always. And when he did, people looked at me like I was the one causing all the trouble, you know. They always do. I guess this is because I'm older.

When I grow up and have kids I'm not gonna ask the older ones to take care of the little guys. No way! Nobody should have to look after weasels.

WORK SHEET

_____

_____

_____

_____

_____

_____

_____

_____

_____

_____

_____

EDWARD

Ed finds his older sister's behavior off the wall.

Around our house the phone is always ringing. And most of the calls are for my teenage sister, Diane. She gets calls from her girlfriends all the time, or she calls them, and all they do is talk about a lot of stupid junk. Like about cute clothes and cute boys and dance lessons and parties and about other kids and how they're jerks and stuff. And they giggle a lot and say, "Ya know, ya know," over and over. Just listening to them makes you wanna puke.

Last week it seemed like all of the calls were about Bobby Lawrence and about how cool he was and how he wore cool clothes and lived in a cool house. Cool cool, cool. The say "Cool," a lot, too. Anyway, Diane talked about Bobby Lawrence being cute and how she really liked him and how she was really bummed out because he never ever talked to her or anything. Hey, can you blame him? Who wants to talk to someone who says "Cool" all the time?

Then, guess what? Bobby Lawrence called her up yesterday. And do you know what? She goes and treats him awful. Yeah, after all week talking about how cool he was and everything, she goes and acts like some stuck-up jerk.

You know, I sometimes think maybe girls are goofed up in the head.

WORK SHEET

WILLIAM

The domestic scene isn't as smooth now that Mother is working.

My mom went to work because she and Dad thought this way we would have more money. But now that she isn't home a lot of the time, Dad and I have to do a whole bunch of housework. Which I hate. I can't stand dusting and running the sweeper and cleaning and straightening up all of the time. It's the pits.

Before Mom went to work, I used to have time to mess around and play and watch TV. Now, I'm always doing some kind of stupid work. And it seems like it never gets done. I mean, just as soon as you dust something a whole bunch of new dust comes along. It's like there's this dust fairy coming around and trashing everything every five minutes or something. And the wastebaskets fill up again right away and the rug gets messed up right away and. . . . Hey, it's like you can't ever get finished, you know.

The worst part of Mom working is that now Dad cooks us dinner sometimes. Wow, does he ever know how to ruin food! He can't even fix canned soup so it tastes right. Last night he fixed these grilled cheese sandwiches that tasted like Elmer's Glue spread on burned toast. Yuck-ola.

You know what? I think things were a whole lot neater before we had so much money.

WORK SHEET

_____

_____

_____

_____

_____

_____

_____

_____

_____

_____

_____

CLARK

Adult behavior is often not exemplary.

I think about grownups a lot. About how they live and work and the stuff they do. And sometimes I think that maybe they aren't very happy. I mean, when you look at the news on TV and hear about what grownups are doing all over the world you sometimes wonder if they ever stop fighting and arguing and causing trouble.

Even though kids fight and argue they don't wind up hating each other forever and doing stupid stuff that messes everything up, you know. They just yell at each other and say off-the-wall stuff and push each other around and then make up and go on like always, like nothing ever happened. But, for some reason, older people can't seem to do this.

Like my family—when they get together they argue over the dumbest stuff you've ever heard of and scream and yell at each other like a bunch of goons. Last Sunday, when they started in arguing after dinner, my dog started in barking like crazy. So, I took him over to the vacant lot and we jumped around on some old boards. You could tell he was glad to be out of the house.

Sometimes, I think my dog makes a lot more sense than grownups any day.

WORK SHEET

DANNY

Danny doesn't enjoy visiting the dentist.

Every now and then I have to go to the dentist. Even though my teeth are okay. My mom and dad say it's a good idea to get used to going when you're little because it's something you have to do for the rest of your life. I don't think this is the reason at all. I think the reason they make you go is because this is another way of getting even with kids.

I hate my dentist. His name is Doctor Miller and he's a creep. Even though he acts real nice, you know he's a creep because he's got all this weird stuff in his office that he just can't wait to use. He's just being nice now so you'll come back when you have a toothache or something. Then it'll be different. Then he'll drill your head off.

And he's got this awful breath, too. Yuck. It makes me sick when he gets in my face. For two cents, I'd bite his fingers. But I can't because my mom is always there watching me like a hawk. And after we leave the dentist's office she always says, "Now, that wasn't so bad, was it?" How does she know? She didn't have to sit there with this creep's big huge fingers pulling her mouth all out of shape.

I don't care what anybody says; I think dentists are a bunch of rats.

ORDER DIRECT

MONOLOGUES THEY HAVEN'T HEARD, Karshner. Modern speeches written in the language of today. $7.95.

MORE MONOLOGUES THEY HAVEN'T HEARD, Karshner. More exciting living-language speeches. $7.95.

SCENES THEY HAVEN'T SEEN, Karshner. Fresh, contemporary scenes for men and women. $7.95.

FOR WOMEN, MONOLOGUES THEY HAVEN'T HEARD, Pomerance. Contemporary speeches for actresses. $7.95

MONOLOGUES FOR KIDS, Roddy. 28 wonderful speeches for boys and girls. $7.95.

MORE MONOLOGUES for KIDS, Roddy. More great speeches for boys and girls. $7.95.

SCENES FOR KIDS, Roddy. 30 scenes for girls and boys. $7.95.

MONOLOGUES FOR TEENAGERS, Karshner. Contemporary speeches written in language that is *now.* $7.95.

SCENES FOR TEENAGERS, Karshner. Scenes for today's teen boys and girls. $7.95.

HIGH SCHOOL MONOLOGUES THEY HAVEN'T HEARD, Karshner. Contemporary speeches for high schoolers, $7.95.

DOWN HOME MONOLOGUES, Karshner. Speeches for men and women in the language of rural America. $7.95.

MONOLOGUES FROM THE CLASSICS, ed. Karshner. Speeches from Shakespeare, Marlowe and others. An excellent collection for men and women, $7.95.

SCENES FROM THE CLASSICS, ed. Maag. Scenes from Shakespeare and others. $7.95.

MONOLOGUES FROM RESTORATION PLAYS, ed. Maag. A ready reference to great speeches from the period. $7.95.

SHAKESPEARE'S MONOLOGUES THEY HAVEN'T HEARD, ed. Dotterer. Lesser known speeches from The Bard. $7.95.

MONOLOGUES FROM CHEKHOV, trans. Cartwright. Modern translations from Chekhov's major plays: *Cherry Orchard, Uncle Vanya, Three Sisters, The Sea Gull.* $7.95.

MONOLOGUES FROM GEORGE BERNARD SHAW, ed. Michaels. Great speeches for men and women from the works of G.B.S. $7.95.

MONOLOGUES FROM OSCAR WILDE, ed. Michaels. The best of Wilde's urbane, dramatic writing from his greatest plays. For men and women. $7.95.

WOMAN, Susan Pomerance. Monologues for actresses. $7.95.

WORKING CLASS MONOLOGUES, Karshner. Speeches from blue collar occupations. Waitress, cleaning lady, policewoman, truck driver, miner, etc. $7.95.

MODERN SCENES FOR WOMEN, Pomerance. Modern scenes for today's versatile actresses. $7.95.

MONOLOGUES FROM MOLIERE, trans. Dotterer. A definitive collection of speeches from the French Master. The first translation into English prose. $7.95.

SHAKESPEARE'S MONOLOGUES FOR WOMEN, trans. Dotterer. $7.95.

DIALECT MONOLOGUES, Karshner/Stern. 13 essential dialects applied to contemporary monologues. Book and Cassette Tape. $19.95.

YOU SAID A MOUTHFUL, Karshner. Tongue twisters galore. Great exercises for actors, singers, public speakers. Fun for everyone. $7.95.

TEENAGE MOUTH, Karshner. Modern monologues for young men and women. $7.95.

SHAKESPEARE'S LADIES, Dotterer. A second book of Shakespeare's monologues for women. With a descriptive text on acting Shakespeare. $7.95.

BETH HENLEY:MONOLOGUES FOR WOMEN, Henley. *Crimes of the Heart* and others. $7.95.

CITY WOMEN, Smith. 20 powerful, urban monologues. Great audition pieces. $7.95.

Your check or money order (no cash or COD) plus handling charges of $2.50 for the first book, and $1.50 for each additional book. California residents add 8.25 %. Send orders to: Dramaline Publications, 10470 Riverside Drive, Suite #201, Toluca Lake, CA 91602.